SPOTTYSAURUS TELLS THE TRUTH

A book about being a good friend
and telling the truth

DINO MANOLI

Spottysaurus was a dinosaur.

A fabulous blue dinosaur with a long blue neck, a huge blue belly and beautiful yellow eyes.

Spottysaurus was, in fact, blue all over, apart from one big bright pink spot on her back.

That big spot is why she was a Spottysaurus, but all her dinosaur friends called her Spot.

One day, Spot was playing with her friend Barry.

They had been out together exploring in the forest for ages and were now starting to feel a little tired.

They found a nice spot under a shady tree to settle down and nap.

Barry slowly swung his neck around his body and curled up.

He took his glasses off, put them gently by his side, closed his eyes and eventually fell asleep.

Spot fidgeted about a little. She just couldn't get comfy.

Although she was tired, she just couldn't fall asleep.

She sighed, looked around and noticed Barry's glasses.

"Oooo!" Spot said herself. "I wonder what it would be like to wear them? It might be fun; I could pretend to be Barry."

Spot thought to herself and giggled.

She carefully tiptoed over, picked them up and slipped them on.

They were rather too large for her face and everything looked blurry.

Spot started to feel a little dizzy.

She wobbled to her left, then wobbled to her right and then wobbled forward so much that she fell.

Landing with a big, and rather painful, thump!

Spot sat up, she felt a bit sore "No bumps or cuts." she said to herself.

Looking around, she gasped as Barry's glasses had snapped in two.

Spot suddenly felt very hot and very scared.

She carefully lifted both pieces and put them next to Barry.

She lay down and shut her eyes tightly.

As she lay still, she felt some dinosaurs walk past with big, heavy stomps, which made the ground shake… Barry gradually woke up from his sleep.

"What a lovely nap," he announced loudly.

Barry reached for his glasses and gasped as he saw they were broken.

Barry started to cry.

Spot tried to comfort her friend.

She was very sad and knew she should tell the truth about what happened.

Spot opened her mouth to explain what she had done, but she was scared.

After a while, Taylor the Triceratops came along and saw that Barry was upset.

"What's wrong, Barry?" he asked, worried about his friend.

"My glasses have been snapped while I was having a nap," he said sadly.

"Do you know what happened?

"I walked by earlier and saw they were broken," replied Taylor.

"I wondered what happened but didn't want to wake you and Spot up. Can we fix them?"

Barry shook his head and looked sadly at his glasses, and off Taylor stomped.

Spot didn't say anything.

After a while, Spike the Stegosaurus came by and saw that Barry was upset.

"What's wrong, Barry?" he asked, worried about his friend.

"My glasses have been snapped while I was having a nap," he said sadly.

"Do you know what happened?

"I walked by earlier and saw they were broken," replied Spike.

"I wondered what happened but didn't want to wake you and Spot up. Can we fix them?"

Barry shook his head and looked sadly at his glasses, and off Spike stomped.

Spot took a deep breath.

"It was me," She said nervously.

"I'm so sorry, Barry. It was an accident"

Barry looked at his friend, confused.

Spot explained what had happened, how she had tried them on, felt dizzy and wobbly and fallen over.

Barry thought for a minute.

"Thank you for telling me the truth, Spot.

I never knew you wanted to try my glasses on."

He looked up and smiled "Did they really make you go all wobbly?"

"Very, very wobbly," she chuckled "So wobbly I fell over!" and with that they both laughed.

"I'm so glad you told me the truth, Spot. You're my best friend".

"Me too!" Spot agreed.

"I was scared you'd be angry at me, even though it was an accident."

"Best friends should always tell each other the truth."
Barry smiled.

Can you walk home with me, please, so I can wear my spare glasses?"

"Of course I can Barry. And I promise not to get all wobbly and fall over again."

Both friends laughed and slowly walked back home together to help Barry find his spare glasses.

Story Activity Time

Point to which 2 friends played together and then fell asleep in the forest?

Story Activity Time

Point to the 2 Dinosaurs that didn't want to wake Barry up when he was asleep.

Story Activity Time

Which dinosaur was very sad that his glasses were broken?

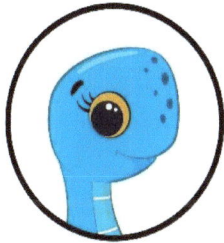

Story Activity Time

Which dinosaur was very brave and told the truth?

30

www.ingramcontent.com/pod-product-compliance
Lightning Source LLC
Chambersburg PA
CBHW041241020426
42333CB00002B/36